GW01403046

Slips and trips

Guidance for employers
on identifying hazards
and controlling risks

HSG 155

HSE BOOKS

© Crown copyright 1996

Applications for reproduction should be made in writing to:
Copyright Unit, Her Majesty's Stationery Office,
St Clements House, 2-16 Colegate, Norwich NR3 1BQ

First published 1996
Reprinted 1999, 2001, 2002

ISBN 0 7176 1145 0

This guidance is issued by the Health and Safety Executive. Following this
guidance is not compulsory and you are free to take other action. But if
you do follow the guidance you will normally be doing enough to comply
with the law. Health and safety inspectors seek to secure compliance with
the law and may refer to this guidance as illustrating good practice.

Contents

Introduction

1   Slips and trips, together with resulting falls, are the main cause of major injuries at work. This guidance aims to help reduce those incidents and injuries. It explains how anyone at work, but particularly employers, can through good management and risk assessment reduce slip and trip hazards. Some business sectors, for example food and catering, each year report higher than average slip and trip injuries. The Health and Safety Executive (HSE) has also produced specific guidance on slip and trip hazards for some sectors of business where there is a higher risk (see Appendix 3 for details).

The single most common cause of a non-fatal major injury to employees in 1993/94 was a slip, trip or fall on the same level (36%)

Legal duties

2   Health and safety legislation includes duties to prevent or control slip and trip risks. These are mainly aimed at employers and others who have some control, such as owners and landlords. Employees also have some duties and may find this guidance helpful.

3   The principal duties are:

■ The **Health and Safety at Work etc Act 1974** (HSW Act) which places a duty on employers to ensure the health and safety of employees and others who may be affected by their work activities.

Employees are required not to endanger themselves or others and to use any safety equipment provided by their employer. The HSW Act also places a general duty on manufacturers, suppliers etc to make sure that their products are safe and without risk to health or safety and that they give adequate information about using the product.

- The **Management of Health and Safety at Work Regulations 1999** build on the HSW Act and include duties for people in control of workplaces to assess risks (including slip and trip risks). They require appropriate arrangements for effective planning, organisation, control, monitoring and review of any measures to safeguard health and safety identified by the risk assessment.

- The **Workplace (Health, Safety and Welfare) Regulations 1992** require floors to be suitable, in good condition and free of obstructions. Traffic routes should be organised so that people can circulate safely.

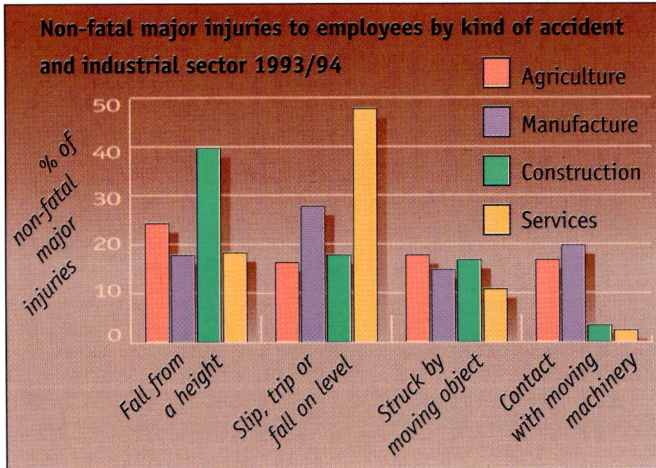

Non-fatal major injuries to employees by kind of accident and industrial sector 1993/94

Scale and costs

4 The numbers and costs of slip and trip accidents are high:

- to the **individual** in lost income, pain suffered and reduced quality of life;
- to the **employer** in damages, administration and insurance costs, lost production and temporary absences from work;
- to **society** with a loss of potential output, medical costs, social security, etc.

*Major injuries to employees caused by a slip, trip or fall on the same level
1986/87 - 1993/94 (as reported to all enforcement authorities)*

	1986/87	87/88	88/89	89/90	90/91	91/92	92/93	93/94
Major injuries caused by slip, trip or fall	5480	5452	5563	5852	6396	5628	5513	5962
Slip, trip or fall as a proportion of all major injuries	26%	27%	28%	29%	32%	32%	33%	36%

5   Slips and trips are common in all business sectors and are the main cause of reported major injuries. Many would have been avoided if employers more actively controlled the hazards that contributed to them.

6   In 1993/94 over 33 000 slip, trip and fall injuries were reported to HSE and local authorities. Some left people unable to work for long periods and some even killed people.

7   Reported slip and trip injuries vary between business sectors. The highest are food, drink and tobacco, followed by the repair of consumer goods and vehicles.

8   Such injuries can happen to anyone, regardless of age or sex. Older people, particularly women, are often injured more severely.

9   Civil proceedings and compensation claims can be costly and damage a company's reputation, particularly where the public are involved, for example in shopping centres.

10   At 1993/94 values slip and trip accidents are estimated to have cost employers £300 million per year, made up of damage costs, extra production costs, administration and insurance costs. The estimated cost to society is between £810-£840 million a year.

11   Effective solutions are often simple, cheap and lead to savings and other benefits.

In 1993/94 slips, trips and falls on the same level were the most common cause of non-fatal major injuries in both the manufacturing sector (27%) and service sector (48%)

Managing health and safety

12 Proper health and safety management will help you to analyse problems, decide what to do, put decisions into practice and check that actions have been effective.

PLANNING: Put in place a system which identifies priorities and sets targets for improvement. Whenever possible, remove risks or minimise them by using control measures, for example careful selection of equipment and working practices which prevent or contain hazards.

ORGANISATION: To secure a progressive improvement in reducing the number of slips and trips, workers will need to be involved and committed. Give individuals (for example supervisors) responsibilities, to ensure that their areas of the workplace are kept clean and tidy. Keep a record of who is responsible for what arrangements. Make these details clear to everyone.

CONTROL: Ensure and promote health and safety as planned, for example by checking that work processes are being carried out correctly. Keep a record of cleaning and maintenance work etc.

MONITORING AND REVIEW: Secure progressive improvement by reviewing your approach in the light of experience. Look at accident investigation and inspection reports. Do they show an improvement? Discuss slip and trip risks with any safety representatives.

Where you employ five or more people, you should keep a record of your arrangements.

13 The management of risks from slips and trips should be the same as for any other hazard. A tried and tested method is described in the HSE leaflet *Five steps to successful health and safety management* (see Appendix 3 for details). This is summarised next.

Case study 1

Following a number of slips in the kitchen of one of the hotels in a large hotel chain, the employer, safety advisor and staff decided to co-operate to reduce this problem during their monthly staff consultative committee. The problem was investigated and it was found that the two main issues were waiting staff rushing to receive orders and spillages left on the floor.

The consultative committee raised awareness of the problem by showing the trend in accidents on a graph posted in staff areas, encouraging staff not to run, and to clean up spillages immediately. The following month there were no accidents in this area.

Assessing slip and trip risks

14 All employers are required to assess risks to employees and others who may be affected by their work. This helps the employer find out what needs to be done to satisfy legal duties. There are no fixed rules about how a risk assessment should be carried out, but there are general principles that should be followed. HSE recommend a five step approach.

STEP 1: Look for hazards. Look around the workplace (including outdoor areas) for anything that may be a slip or trip hazard, such as poor floor surfaces, loose carpets, etc.

A HAZARD is anything that can cause harm

STEP 2: Decide who might be harmed and how. Consider who will come into the workplace and whether they are at risk.

STEP 3: Evaluate the risks. Consider the precautions already taken and assess whether they adequately deal with the risks.

STEP 4: Record your findings. If you have five or more employees you should record the significant findings.

STEP 5: Review assessment from time to time. If there is any significant change you should review the risk assessment to make sure that precautions are still adequate.

A RISK is the chance or likelihood of someone being harmed by a hazard

15 For employees who work away from the workplace the risk assessment should include consideration of the hazards and risks they may encounter so that appropriate training, footwear, etc can be provided.

Case study 2

A shop worker was injured while measuring material in the factory shop. She stepped back to unroll material on a table and tripped over a weighing scale located directly behind. She suffered a fractured wrist in the fall.

Reorganising the tables or relocating the scales was possible and proper planning would have prevented this accident. The employer's risk assessment should have identified this hazard. The employer also failed to make clear whose responsibility it was to ensure safety in that area of the workplace.

16 Slip and trip accidents may have different causes, but often have the same result. By looking at the contributing factors separately, it is possible to work out more accurately the cause of a slip or trip accident.

- Slips occur when the foot and floor surface cannot make effective contact/grip, usually caused when something has been spilt or when the shoe sole and floor are unsuited.

Slip hazards	Spills and splashes of liquids and solids
	Wet floors (following cleaning)
	Unsuitable footwear
	Loose mats on polished floors
	Rain, sleet and snow
	Change from a wet to a dry surface (footwear still wet)
	Unsuitable floor surface/ covering
	Dusty floors
	Sloping surfaces

Trip hazards	Loose floorboards/tiles
	Loose and worn mats/carpets
	Uneven outdoor surfaces
	Holes/cracks
	Changes in surface level - ramps, steps and stairs
	Cables across walking areas
	Obstructions
	Bumps, ridges and protruding nails etc
	Low wall and floor fixtures - door catches, door stops,
	Electrical and telephone socket outlets

Factors which increase risk	Organisation of walkways
	Badly placed mirrors/reflections from glazing
	Poor or unsuitable lighting
	Wrong cleaning regime/materials
	Moving goods/carrying/pushing or pulling a load
	Rushing around
	Distractions/fatigue
	Effects of alcohol

■ Trips occur when an obstruction prevents normal movement of the foot, resulting in a loss of balance. Usually caused by objects on the floor or due to uneven surfaces.

Managing risks

17 There are many simple measures that can be taken to eliminate or reduce risks. The following table gives some suggestions.

Hazard	Suggested action
Spillage of wet and dry substances	Clean spills up immediately. If a liquid is greasy ensure a suitable cleaning agent is used.
	After cleaning the floor may be wet for some time. Use appropriate signs to tell people the floor is still wet and arrange alternative bypass routes.
Trailing cables	Position equipment to avoid cables crossing pedestrian routes, use cable covers to securely fix to surfaces, restrict access to prevent contact.
Miscellaneous rubbish, for example plastic bags	Keep areas clear, remove rubbish and do not allow to build up.
Rugs/mats	Ensure mats are securely fixed and do not have curling edges.
Slippery surfaces	Assess the cause and treat accordingly, for example treat chemically, appropriate cleaning method etc.
Change from wet to dry floor surface	Suitable footwear, warn of risks by using signs, locate doormats where these changes are likely.
Poor lighting	Improve lighting levels and placement of light fittings to ensure more even lighting of all floor areas.
Changes of level	Improve lighting, add apparent tread nosings.
Slopes	Improve visibility, provide hand rails, use floor markings.
Smoke/steam obscuring view	Eliminate or control by redirecting it away from risk areas; improve ventilation and warn of it.
Unsuitable footwear	Ensure workers choose suitable footwear, particularly with the correct type of sole.
	If the type of work requires special protective footwear the employer is required by law to provide it free of charge.

Good housekeeping

18 Get workplace conditions right in the first place. It will make tackling slip and trip risks easier. Choose the right floor surfaces and suitable lighting, properly plan pedestrian and traffic routes and avoid overcrowding. All these are important.

19 Good housekeeping is important in preventing hazards and applies as much to offices and commercial premises as to factories and workshops, etc. Keep work areas tidy. It will create a better working environment and mean fewer accidents.

20 Properly train workers, particularly in the correct use of any safety and cleaning equipment provided, and clearly state who is responsible for what; this will help to minimise risks.

21 Ensure that cleaning methods and equipment are suitable for the type of surface being treated. These depend on several factors, such as the type of use and location and will have been identified in the risk assessment. Take care not to create additional slip and trip risks, for example from residues not properly removed from a surface. More information on cleaning is given in Appendix 1.

22 A proper programme of maintenance will ensure that the steps you have taken remain effective.

23 Necessary maintenance and repairs must be carried out. You may need to get outside help or guidance from a specialist, for example a flooring manufacturer or supplier.

24 While cleaning and maintenance work is being carried out, take care to avoid creating new hazards. Fence off wet surfaces until dry, take care with trailing leads from cleaning

Case study 3

An experienced bench worker slipped on a dusty floor in the training area of the factory. He recieved torn ligaments in his right hand when he put his arm out to steady himself. He needed treatment for his injuries and several days' working time was lost.

This company have now reviewed housekeeping procedures and as a result will purchase industrial cleaning equipment. They have also made contract cleaning arrangements with a specialist company.

equipment, if possible carry out cleaning and maintenance during quieter hours.

25 A good system of maintenance ensures that:

- maintenance (including inspection, testing, adjustment and cleaning) is carried out at suitable intervals;
- dangerous defects are corrected and access to faulty equipment or hazardous areas is prevented in the meantime;
- suitable records are kept so that the system can be monitored.

Lighting

26 Lighting should enable people to see obstructions on floors, potentially slippery areas etc so they can work safely. Replace, repair or clean lights before lighting levels become insufficient for safe working.

27 Arrange lighting and light fittings so they do not to create dazzling light or glare that can make it difficult to see. Ensure light levels are not reduced, for example by goods stacked in such a way as to block light or cast shadows.

28 Local lighting should always be provided at staircases and changes of level; it is usually also needed at ramps where there is no change in colour, texture or flooring material from level walkway to ramp.

Flooring

29 Poor floor conditions are a major cause of slips and trips. Regular checks should be made for loose floor finishes, holes and cracks in surfaces, loose and worn out rugs and mats, etc.

30 Even a good surface will become dangerous in certain conditions, for example if liquids are spilt onto it. Ideally,

Case study 4

A paperboard machine operative tripped over an electricity supply cable trailing on the ground. The cable was one of a number temporarily in place because contractors were working at the premises. The operative damaged her knee in the accident.

Although the work being carried out was temporary, the company had not properly assessed the new risks created by this additional work, therefore failing to ensure that precautions to prevent or control the hazards were still adequate.

13

Case study 5

A worker tripped over a trailing air hose left in an alleyway. The hose had not been put away after use. The alleyway was poorly lit and the incident occurred at night. Following an investigation the company have installed flood-lighting in poorly lit areas and have relocated the airline and hose. Safety awareness and good housekeeping training is now given to all staff.

working practices and machinery should be arranged to prevent spills. However, where they do occur they should be cleaned up immediately or the area fenced off to make people aware until they can be cleaned up. Where floors are unavoidably wet or dusty through work activity, take special care in the choice of floor coverings or floor surface.

Obstructions

31   Failure to tidy up properly and objects left on walkways can easily go unnoticed and cause a fall. Where it is not possible to remove obstacles, take precautions to reduce the risk of accident by preventing access, or warning people of the dangers, for example by using warning signs or hazard cones.

Footwear

32   While much can be done to reduce hazards, there will often be some remaining risk. An important second line of defence will be to ensure people have the right footwear.

33   To ensure the safety of their workers, employers have a duty to provide, free of charge, all necessary personal protective equipment, including safety footwear.

34   Footwear should:
- be appropriate for the task and floor surfaces;
- fit properly;
- be maintained or renewed as necessary.

More information on footwear is given in Appendix 2.

Case study 6

A railway company were concerned at the number of slipping and falling accidents on the terrazzo floor of a station concourse.

They engaged contractors to undertake a proprietary treatment process. This involved diamond grinding to produce a perfectly flat surface, followed by the application of a protective and slip-resistant coating.

The treatment and a modified cleaning regime has resulted in a surface which has a greatly enhanced appearance and which is subjectively and demonstrably more slip-resistant. In addition, during the 18 month period following treatment no civil claims arose from slips on the concourse compared with an average, previously, of three or four per year.

The railway company were so impressed with the overall improvements at the station that the terrazzo floors of other stations in the area have now been similarly treated.

A P P E N D I X 1
Floors

1   Floor surfaces are often chosen because they look good, are easy to clean or are inexpensive. However, there are other factors which are just as, if not more important. When selecting a surface it is important to take into account the following:

- location - indoors or outdoors;
- who will use the floor and how often;
- demands made on the floor surfaces by heavy vehicular traffic such as fork lift trucks or heavy pedestrian traffic found in transport interchanges, shopping malls etc;
- likely contamination from work processes;
- exposure to excesses of temperature;
- the properties of the surface itself;
- how it will be cleaned and how often;
- other legal requirements, eg Food Hygiene Legislation;
- maintenance;
- the anticipated static loading on the floors from stored goods, filing cabinets etc.

2   In general, rougher floors have better slip resistance, especially in wet conditions. It is not true that to be kept hygienically clean, a floor must be smooth. More cleaning effort may be needed, but there is no need to put up with a slippery smooth floor because it is more hygienic or easier to clean.

3   Some combinations of shoe sole and flooring materials have been found to be less slippery than others. These are given in a table shown at Appendix 2. The information was compiled from various sources which are listed at Appendix 3.

4   A number of British and European standards contain useful guidance on suitable floor surfaces for particular situations and how they should be laid. This information is available from the British Standards Institution (see Appendix 3).

Measuring slipperiness

5 A number of devices are available for measuring the slipperiness of floor surfaces. They usually work by measuring the friction between a test pad (commonly made of hard rubber) and the surface being tested.

6 These devices use various methods to bring the test pad into contact with the surface, and their limitations need to be realised and appreciated particularly in relation to the method of measurement, what is actually measured and the relevance of the figure obtained to the degree of slip hazard. Testers may estimate:

- static friction - the force needed to start one surface sliding over another;
- dynamic friction - the force needed to maintain slipping;
- a combination of the two.

The 'coefficient of friction' (static or dynamic) is a measure of the resistance to slipping, **zero** indicating perfect sliding (ie no slip-resistance), **one** indicating a frictional force equal to that keeping the surfaces together, eg the weight of a standing person. The coefficients of friction for any pair of surfaces will rarely be the same and the dynamic coefficient will vary with the relative velocity of the surfaces.

7 Consideration should be given to the meaning of results gained from:

- using a particular test pad;
- the velocity of movement;

- the type of footwear that will come into contact with the floor;
- the expected type of movement.

8 The variety of circumstances found in any workplace mean it is not feasible to specify a limiting value for floor friction above which a slip hazard would not exist. Quoted friction values should be interpreted with caution and it is advisable to establish which test method was used. Do not simply put your trust in a number!

Improving slip-resistance

9 If slipping and tripping becomes a problem with existing floors it may be possible to treat the floor in some way rather than replace it.

10 The following techniques may help:
- abrading or chemical treatment of concrete to give a roughened finish;
- coating with a resin containing abrasive particles;
- overlaying with a flooring material containing abrasive particles or a textured surface;
- using adhesive-backed flooring strips or squares.

11 When treating an existing floor as suggested above, check to make sure that any new flooring and adhesive materials are compatible with the intended surface. Before treating a concrete floor, oil and grease deposits should be removed so that the new surfacing will adhere properly and not deteriorate unduly.

12 Flooring materials must be laid carefully in accordance with manufacturers' instructions by competent persons where appropriate. Care should be taken to avoid curling edges of flooring material, especially sheet vinyl, loose tiles etc.

13 Appropriate safety precautions should be taken when laying or treating floors. Consult manufacturers' or suppliers' instructions and data sheets for details.

14 Sheet flooring must be laid on a smooth, sound, flat surface. Imperfections will cause uneven and excessive wear and can result in cracking and bubbling. It is preferable not to have joints in sheet flooring. Ideally the seams should be welded, particularly where hygiene is important, such as in hospitals. Welded seams prevent the collection of dirt and make cleaning easier while removing the risk of water getting under the covering and causing lifting. Epoxy resin coatings might be used in an attempt to hide defects, but eventually cracking will occur with movement or deterioration of the base.

15 Anti-slip treatments are usually acid-based and work by etching or roughening the surface. With acid etching it is necessary to remove all the acid as the residue may eventually eat into the concrete, structural steel work, plant or machinery.

16 Depending on how much the floor is used, this treatment wears away, sometimes very quickly. The treatment may have to be applied regularly as part of the cleaning routine.

17 Individual anti-slip treatments are not suitable for all floor types and if not applied correctly may make a floor more slippery. Anti-slip strips may prove impractical if they pick up dirt, hence losing grip while becoming difficult to clean.

Staircases

18 Take special care with stairs. Where possible the steps should be the same depth and height for safe and easy climbing (building regulations say that this must be the case for all new and re-furbished buildings). A handrail must be provided on at least one side of the staircase and be secure.

19 You can improve the slip resistance of stairs by:

- sprinkling the surface of concrete stairs with Carborundum (where it is workable, ie not set) and trowelling it in as the concrete sets;
- cutting grooves parallel to the edges of the treads and infilling with inserts of abrasive material;
- applying specially made 'non-slip' nosings.

20 British and European Standards give more details on the design and construction of stairs, including advice on minimising slip and trip hazards. For further information see British Standards Institution in Appendix 3.

Care, cleaning and maintenance

21 Correct floor care involving cleaning, and sealing or polishing will:

- reduce slip hazards;
- increase the life of the floor;
- help prevent health hazards;
- save money.

22 What is good for one floor surface may not be so for another. Many workplaces have more than one type of flooring. A record of each type of flooring and the makers' recommendations on their care will help ensure each type is treated correctly. Cleaning personnel should be adequately trained, particularly where mechanical aids are used.

23 The correct cleaning methods to use will depend on the type of spills or dirt to be removed.

Cleaning advice

24 Chemical cleaner must be completely washed away with clean water and floors dried. Residues of detergents can cause slip hazards and may react with other chemicals used later.

25 Accessible floors that are hand washed or mopped should not be left overly wet.

26 Some powered cleaning machines will wash and dry in one operation. The type of application pads or brushes used can affect the end result, for example rotary brushes may leave a build-up of deposits in the joints of a tiled floor increasing the danger of slipping. Regular checks of both machinery and floor surfaces will help to identify such problems.

27 Polish should be the correct type for the surface to be treated (fully buffable, semi-buffable or dry bright). The maker's instructions on its use should be followed. Fully buffable polished surfaces need periodic rebuffing to maintain a good sheen and to remove wax deposits that would otherwise cause a slipping hazard.

28 Ideally floors should be cleaned outside main working hours or at times when people and traffic are at a minimum. If after cleaning floors they are still wet, barriers and warning signs should be used and remain in place until the floor is safe to walk over, allowing for drying time etc. Signs should conform to the Health and Safety (Safety Signs and Safety Signal) Regulations 1996. Where a corridor or gangway cannot be completely closed off during cleaning, it is better for half its width to be cleaned or treated at a time.

Maintenance

29 Prompt action is necessary to protect people from the danger of tripping or slipping on worn, damaged or defective flooring. The affected area may need to be closed off with barriers and signs until permanent repairs can be done.

30 When repair work is being carried out, precautions similar to those outlined for cleaning should be observed to ensure the safety of passers-by. The people doing the repairs should have sufficient knowledge to enable them to do the job competently and in safety as some materials used may be hazardous. It may be necessary to get guidance from the flooring maker or supplier, or to call in a specialist contractor.

31 Further details on cleaning and treatment of floors are available in a number of British and European Standards, available from the British Standards Institution, see Appendix 3.

Footwear

1 British and European Standards for safety footwear do not include test specifications for slip resistance. Safety footwear is not designed primarily to protect the wearer from slipping. Its main aim is to protect the foot from falling objects, protruding nails, etc.

2 Choosing suitable footwear to prevent slips needs care. Different characteristics are needed for different conditions. The sole of the footwear will work in much the same way as a car tyre ie:

- On **wet** surfaces the sole should have a well defined pattern (tread) as more edges will give a firmer grip. The tread will cut through surface liquid and break up the slippery layer under foot.
- On **dry** surfaces it is better to have as much of the sole as possible in contact with the ground so the pattern on the sole is less important.

3 It is not possible to make firm recommendations about soling materials as none will perform well in all conditions. The best approach is to test a range of footwear under actual working conditions to find which is best in the particular circumstances. New soles may have a skin or film on them from the moulding or forming process. Once this has worn off the anti-slip performance of the soles will change. Footwear should therefore be tried over a period of time.

4 Some combinations of shoe sole and flooring materials have been found to be less slippery than others. The table opposite may help with the choice of footwear.

Shoe sole material and floor types

Slip resistance of combinations

Normal floor conditions	Floor types	Shoe sole materials		
		PVC and leather	Urethane and rubbers	Microcellular urethane and rubbers
Smooth	Stainless steel	Most slippery	Most slippery	Less slippery
↓	Polished ceramic	Most slippery	Most slippery	Less slippery
↓	Polished wood	Most slippery	Most slippery	Less slippery
↓	Smooth resin	Most slippery	Most slippery	Less slippery
Matt	Matt ceramic	Most slippery	Less slippery	Less slippery
↓	Terrazzo	Most slippery	Less slippery	Least slippery
↓	PVC/vinyl	Less slippery	Less slippery	Least slippery
↓	Concrete	Less slippery	Least slippery	Least slippery
Rough	Paving stones	Less slippery	Least slippery	Least slippery

Relative slip resistance of combinations of shoes and floors in water-wet conditions

Key:
- Most slippery
- Less slippery
- Least slippery

Each floor listed is untreated, is not profiled and is in water-wet conditions. Slipperiness may be increased by other liquids, especially those more viscous than water.

With wear, floors and shoe soles may change, often becoming more slippery. However, microcellular urethanes often remain unchanged with wear.

25

Further Information

Organisations

Health and Safety Laboratory, Broad Lane, Sheffield S3 7HQ,
Tel: 01142 892000

British Standards Institution, 389 Chiswick High Road,
London W4 4AL, Tel: 020 8996 9001

Royal Society for the Prevention of Accidents, RoSPA House,
Edgbaston Park, 353 Bristol Road, Birmingham B5 7ST
Tel: 0121 248 2000

British Retail Consortium, Second Floor, 21 Dartmouth
Street, London SW1H 9BP Tel: 020 7854 8900

Rubber and Plastics Research Association Technology Ltd,
Shawbury, Shrewsbury, Shropshire SY4 4NR Tel: 01939 250383

British Cleaning Council, PO Box 1328, Kidderminster,
Worcestershire DY11 5ZJ, Tel: 01562 851129

Building Research Establishment, Garston, Watford
WD25 9XX, Tel: 01923 664000

Published guidance and research reports

British and European Standards

Details of relevant British and European standards are
available from The British Standards Institution (address
above), these include:

BS 1711 1975 *Specification for solid rubber flooring*

BS EN 649 1997 *Resilient floor coverings*

BS EN 654 1997 *Resilient floor coverings*

BS 8204 Part 3 1993 *Screeds, bases and in situ floorings. Code of practice for polymer modified cementitious wearing surfaces*

BS 8204 Part 4 1993 *Screeds, bases and in situ floorings. Code of practice for terrazzo wearing surfaces*

BS 5378 1982 *Safety signs and colours*
Part 1 1980 *Specification for colour and design*
Part 2 1980 *Specification for colorimetric and photometric properties of materials*
Part 3 1982 *Specification for additional signs to those given in 5378: Part 1*

Guidance

Slips and trips: Guidance for the food processing industry
HSG156 1996 HSE Books ISBN 0 7176 0832 8

Workplace health, safety and welfare. Approved Code of Practice and guidance L24 1992 HSE Books
ISBN 0 7176 0413 6

Management of health and safety at work. Approved Code of Practice and guidance L21 2000 ISBN 0 7176 2488 9

Personal protective equipment at work. Guidance on Regulations L25 1992 HSE Books ISBN 0 7176 0415 2

5 steps to risk assessment INDG163 (rev1) 1998 HSE Free leaflet

Five steps to successful health and safety management INDG132 1992 HSE Free leaflet

Essentials of health and safety at work 1994 HSE Books
ISBN 0 7176 0716 X

HSE priced and free publications are available by mail order from HSE Books (see back cover for details). HSE priced publications are also available from good booksellers.

Research reports and articles

Harris G W and Shaw S R, 1988, Slip resistance of floors, user's opinions, tortus instrument readings and roughness measurements *J Occup. Accid* 9 1988 no 4, 287-298

Holah J, 1994, Hygiene and safety in the food industry; Compromise or complementary. Conference proceedings, Paper 7 of *Slipping - Towards safer flooring* 1994 RAPRA ISBN 1 85957 025 9

Manning D P, Jones C and Bruce M, 1986, Slip-resistance on icy surfaces of shoes, crampons and chains - A new machine *J. Occup. Accid* 7 1986 no 4, 273-283

Redfern M S and Bidana B, 1994, Slip resistance of the shoe-floor interface under biomedically-relevant conditions *Ergonomics* 37 1994 no 3, 511-524

While every effort has been made to ensure the accuracy of the references listed in this publication, their future availability cannot be guaranteed.

Printed and published by the Health and Safety Executive C16 9/02